# GIVEN SUGAR, GIVEN SALT

Jane Hirshfield

# GIVEN SUGAR, GIVEN SALT

Perennial

*An Imprint of* HarperCollins*Publishers*

First Perennial edition published 2002.

*Designed and produced by David Bullen Design*

The Library of Congress has catalogued the hardcover edition as follows:
Hirshfield, Jane.
Given sugar, given salt / Jane Hirshfield. —1st ed.
p.   cm.
ISBN 0-06-019954-7
I. Title.
PS3558.I694 G58 2001
811'54—dc21          00-063168

ISBN 0-06-095901-0 (pbk.)
13 14 15  ❖/RRD  15 14 13 12 11

## Acknowledgments

The author is grateful to the editors of those periodicals and anthologies in which some of these poems first appeared:

*Agni*: "Mathematics," "Metempsychosis," "Muslin"; *The American Poetry Review*: "A Hand," "One Life Is Spent, the Other Spends Us," "The Silence," "Waking This Morning Dreamless After Long Sleep"; *The Amicus Journal*: "Tree"; *The Atlantic Monthly*: "Apple"; *The Bark*: "Bone"; *Blue Sofa*: "The Envoy"; *Denver Quarterly*: "Leather," "Minotaur," "Red Onion, Cherries, Boiling Potatoes, Milk—"; *Five Points*: "Button," "Rebus"; *Green Mountains Review*: "Pillow," "A Scale Weighs the Outer World in Pounds and Ounces"; *Hayden's Ferry Review*: "All Summer You Kept Trying to Answer the Knocking," "The Contract"; *Island* (Australia): "A Cedary Fragrance"; *The Kenyon Review*: "Inflection Almost Ungraspable by Grammar," "Poem with Two Endings," "Sleep"; *The Nation*: "Dream Notebook"; *New England Review*: "Dark-Grained, Surprisingly Heavy," "Great Powers Once Raged Through Your Body"; *Northern Lights*: "Clock," "The Gallop"; *The Oxford American*: "Self-Portrait in a Borrowed Cabin," "Walker Evans Interior, 1936"; *Prairie Schooner*: "Moment," "Patched Carpet," "Silk Cord," "Speed and Perfection"; *River City*: "August Day"; *Runes*: "Bobcats, Beetles, Owls"; *Slate*: "All Evening, Each Time I Started to Say It," "Habit"; *The Southern Review*: "Optimism," "The Room"; *The Threepenny Review*: "Always She Reads the Same Translation," "This Was Once a Love Poem"; *Tin House*: "Blue Window," "In Praise of Coldness"; *Wild Duck Review*: "Ink"; *The Yale Review*: "Red Berries."

"In Praise of Coldness" appeared in *Best American Poetry 2001* (New York, Scribner, 2001), edited by Robert Hass, series editor David Lehman, and in *The Pushcart Prize 2002 XXVI* anthology (Wainscott, NY: The Pushcart Press, 2002), edited by Bill Henderson et. al. "The Envoy" also appeared in *Best American Poetry 1999* (New York, Scribner, 1999), edited by Robert Bly, series editor David Lehman. "Dream Notebook" and "Moment" appeared in *American Diaspora: The Poetry of Exile,* edited by Ryan G. Cleave and Virgil Suarez (University of Iowa Press, 2000). "Minotaur," "Moment," and "Speed and Perfection" appeared in *Influence and Mastery,* edited by Stephen Berg (Paul Dry Books, 2000). "Rock" will appear in *Encounters with Earth* (Geological Society of America, 2001) and *Language of the Earth,* edited by Frank H. T. Rhodes and Richard O. Stone (University Reprints, 2001). "Apple" and "The Envoy" were reprinted in *Urthona* (UK), and "The Envoy" was reprinted in *Island* (Australia). A letterpress limited edition of six poems, *Apple & Other Poems,* was published by Brooding Heron Press in spring 2000 to celebrate the inaugural Skagit River Poetry Festival.

## Contents

# GIVEN SUGAR,
# GIVEN SALT

# The Envoy

One day in that room, a small rat.
Two days later, a snake.

Who, seeing me enter,
whipped the long stripe of his
body under the bed,
then curled like a docile house-pet.

I don't know how either came or left.
Later, the flashlight found nothing.

For a year I watched
as something—terror? happiness? grief?—
entered and then left my body.

Not knowing how it came in,
Not knowing how it went out.

It hung where words could not reach it.
It slept where light could not go.
Its scent was neither snake nor rat,
neither sensualist nor ascetic.

There are openings in our lives
of which we know nothing.

Through them
the belled herds travel at will,
long-legged and thirsty, covered with foreign dust.

# Mathematics

I have envied those
who make something
useful, sturdy—
a chair, a pair of boots.

Even a soup,
rich with potatoes and cream.

Or those who fix, perhaps,
a leaking window:
strip out the old cracked putty,
lay down cleanly the line of the new.

You could learn,
the mirror tells me, late at night,
but lacks conviction.
One reflected eyebrow quivers a little.

I look at this
borrowed apartment—
everywhere I question it,
the wallpaper's pattern matches.

Yesterday a woman
showed me
a building shaped
like the overturned hull of a ship,

its roof trusses, under the plaster,
lashed with soaked rawhide,
the columns' marble
painted to seem like wood.
Though possibly it was the other way around?

I look at my unhandy hand,
innocent,
shaped as the hands of others are shaped.
Even the pen it holds is a mystery, really.

*Rawhide*, it writes,
and *chair*, and *marble*.
*Eyebrow.*

Later the woman asked me—
I recognized her then,
my sister, my own young self—

*Does a poem enlarge the world,*
*or only our idea of the world?*

How do you take one from the other,
I lied, or did not lie,
in answer.

# RED BERRIES

Again the pyrocanthus berries redden in rain,
as if return were return.

It is not.

The familiar is not the thing it reminds of.
Today's *yes* is different from yesterday's *yes*.
Even *no*'s adamance alters.

From painting to painting,
century to century,
the tipped-over copper pot spills out different light;
the cut-open beeves,
their caged and muscled display,
are on one canvas radiant, pure; obscene on another.

In the end it is simple enough—

The woman of this morning's mirror
was a stranger
to the woman of last night's;
the passionate dreams of the one who slept
flit empty and thin
from the one who awakens.

One woman washes her face,
another picks up the boar-bristled hairbrush,
a third steps out of her slippers.
That each will die in the same bed means nothing to them.

Our one breath follows another like spotted horses, no two alike.

Black manes and white manes, they gallop.
Piebald and skewbald, eyes flashing sorrow, they too will pass.

# The Room

For two years it lay almost unentered,
almost unoccupied,
except for an insect-hatch of empty cartons.

Then something spiraled,
stirred in a corner, demanded.

And so came the sanding and painting,
the washing of windows,
replacing the cracked half-glass of the door.
So came a bed, a wooden dresser, a desk.

Lain over the dresser's top, a dowry-cloth
from Uzbekistan,
embroidered, cheerful, worn, absurdly expensive.
Before the desk, a chair with woven seat.

The hunt for a rug began.

And during all that time, no idea at all
of why these choices of furniture, this use.
Late, the realization that something was being courted.

And then a small tremble of exhilaration and fear—

for still it was uncertain what was being prepared for,
when the guest would come or in whose shape,
which half-starved, shivering hopes might follow it in.

# APPLE

I woke and remembered
nothing of what I was dreaming.

The day grew light, then dark again—
In all its rich hours, what happened?

A few weeds pulled, a few cold flowers
carried inside for the vase.
A little reading. A little tidying and sweeping.

I had vowed to do nothing I did not wish
to do that day, and kept my promise.

Once, a certain hope came close
and then departed. Passed by me in its familiar
shawl, scented with iodine woodsmoke.

I did not speak to it, nor it to me.
Yet still the habit of warmth traveled
between us, like an apple shared by old friends—

One takes a bite, then the other.
They do this until it is gone.

# A Hand

A hand is not four fingers and a thumb.

Nor is it palm and knuckles,
not ligaments or the fat's yellow pillow,
not tendons, star of the wristbone, meander of veins.

A hand is not the thick thatch of its lines
with their infinite dramas,
nor what it has written,
not on the page,
not on the ecstatic body.

Nor is the hand its meadows of holding, of shaping—
not sponge of rising yeast-bread,
not rotor pin's smoothness,
not ink.

The maple's green hands do not cup
the proliferant rain.
What empties itself falls into the place that is open.

A hand turned upward holds only a single, transparent question.

Unanswerable, humming like bees, it rises, swarms, departs.

# Habit

The shoes put on each time
left first, then right.

The morning potion's teaspoon
of sweetness stirred always
for seven circlings—no fewer, no more—
into the cracked blue cup.

Touching the pocket for wallet,
for keys,
before closing the door.

How did we come
to believe these small rituals' promise,
that we are today the selves we yesterday knew,
tomorrow will be?

How intimate and unthinking,
the way the toothbrush is shaken dry after use,
the part we wash first in the bath.

Which habits we learned from others
and which are ours alone we may never know.
Unbearable to acknowledge
how much they are themselves our fated life.

Open the traveling suitcase—

There the beloved red sweater,
bright tangle of necklace, earrings of amber.
Each confirming: I chose these, I.

But habit is different: it chooses.
And we, its good horse,
opening our mouths at even the sight of the bit.

# REBUS

You work with what you are given,
the red clay of grief,
the black clay of stubbornness going on after.
Clay that tastes of care or carelessness,
clay that smells of the bottoms of rivers or dust.

Each thought is a life you have lived or failed to live,
each word is a dish you have eaten or left on the table.
There are honeys so bitter
no one would willingly choose to take them.
The clay takes them: honey of weariness, honey of vanity,
honey of cruelty, fear.

This rebus—slip and stubbornness,
bottom of river, my own consumed life—
when will I learn to read it
plainly, slowly, uncolored by hope or desire?
Not to understand it, only to see.

As water given sugar sweetens, given salt grows salty,
we become our choices.
Each *yes*, each *no* continues,
this one a ladder, that one an anvil or cup.

The ladder leans into its darkness.
The anvil leans into its silence.
The cup sits empty.

How can I enter this question the clay has asked?

# Waking This Morning
## Dreamless After Long Sleep

But with this sentence:
*"Use your failures for paper."*
Meaning, I understood,
the backs of failed poems, but also my life.

Whose far side I begin now to enter—

A book imprinted without seeming reason,
each blank day bearing on its reverse, in random order,
the mad-set type of another.
December 12, 1960. April 4, 1981. 13th of August, 1974—

Certain words bleed through to the unwritten pages.
To call this memory offers no solace.

*"Even in sleep, the heavy millstones turning."*

I do not know where the words come from,
what the millstones,
where the turning may lead.

I, a woman forty-five, beginning to gray at the temples,
putting pages of ruined paper
into a basket, pulling them out again.

# POEM HOLDING ITS HEART IN ONE FIST

Each pebble in this world keeps
its own counsel.

Certain words—these, for instance—
may be keeping a pronoun hidden.
Perhaps the lover's *you*
or the solipsist's *I*.
Perhaps the philosopher's willowy *it*.

The concealment plainly delights.

Even a desk will gather
its clutch of secret, half-crumpled papers,
eased slowly, over years,
behind the backs of drawers.

Olives adrift in the altering brine-bath
etch onto their innermost pits
a few furrowed salts that will never be found by the tongue.

Yet even with so much withheld,
so much unspoken,
potatoes are cooked with butter and parsley,
and buttons affixed to their sweater.
Invited guests arrive, then dutifully leave.

And this poem, afterward, washes its breasts
with soap and trembling hands, disguising nothing.

# LEATHER

There are times I feel myself cow stripped of her leather.

The hide going on without me,
flensed, vat-dipped, beaten to pliable smoothness.

What remains—awkward, vaguely aware
that something is missing, but what?—continues
its looking outward, evenly breathes.

Sunlight, wind, the black, inquiring noses of others:
sharp now as the knife.

Muscled unjacketed egg.
Impossible butcher's diagram walking. Beginning to graze.

# This Was Once a Love Poem

This was once a love poem,
before its haunches thickened, its breath grew short,
before it found itself sitting,
perplexed and a little embarrassed,
on the fender of a parked car,
while many people passed by without turning their heads.

It remembers itself dressing as if for a great engagement.
It remembers choosing these shoes,
this scarf or tie.

Once, it drank beer for breakfast,
drifted its feet
in a river side by side with the feet of another.

Once it pretended shyness, then grew truly shy,
dropping its head so the hair would fall forward,
so the eyes would not be seen.

It spoke with passion of history, of art.
It was lovely then, this poem.
Under its chin, no fold of skin softened.
Behind the knees, no pad of yellow fat.
What it knew in the morning it still believed at nightfall.
An unconjured confidence lifted its eyebrows, its cheeks.

The longing has not diminished.
Still it understands. It is time to consider a cat,
the cultivation of African violets or flowering cactus.

Yes, it decides:
Many miniature cacti, in blue and red painted pots.

When it finds itself disquieted
by the pure and unfamiliar silence of its new life,
it will touch them—one, then another—
with a single finger outstretched like a tiny flame.

What will become of these
my many lives,
abandoned each morning abruptly to their own fates?

Of the fox who stopped to look up at me,
bright death stippling her muzzle,
and announced—clearly, simply—"I was hungry"?
Of the engine left half-disassembled,
the unmendable roof leaks, the waiting packed bags?

Cloudbellies of horses drinking at sunset.
Fierce embraces remembered half a day if at all.

Even the bedside jar of minute and actual seashells
wavers and thins—
though each was lifted, chosen,
I no longer recall whether in joy or distraction,
in foreknowledge or false belief.

How much more elusive, these half-legible scribblings.
If souvenirs at all, they are someone else's.
As each of my memories,
it seems, is destined to be someone else's,

to belong to a woman who
looks faintly like me and whom I wish well,
as one would any stranger passed in a shop, on the street.

# After Attending Neither the Lecture on How Plants and Animals Self-Orient in Space nor the One on the Abrupt Decline of Frogs

The figure that rides behind her left shoulder is frowning—

*For weeks now, you have been trying to write of*
*the soon-to-be-unremembered:*
*the scent of spirit-duplication ink, the sound of the needle*
*hushing over clear vinyl after the record ends.*
*The winding of watch stems, their sharp, tiny teeth on the thumb.*

*You have collected stories of iceboxes, X rays in shoe stores,*
*of early margarine needing its red dot of dye kneaded in.*

*Nothing has worked.*
*Consider: The bin of your metaphor-making is empty.*
*What care have you taken of me?*

Yes, she admits, it is true.
She is like a dog at the foot of a long-empty tree.
Whatever scent brought her to this, the quarry slipped loose.

That click, click, click of the phonograph needle.
Who, years from now, will know its powerful emotion?
Better to write of the vanishing frogs,
of extinction that matters.

But that moment decades vanished—

the last notes trembling to silence,
the sound of the diamond-tipped needle repeating,
repeating its circles—

to her, it matters.

# BUTTON

It likes both to enter and to leave,
actions it seems to feel as a kind of hide-and-seek.
It knows nothing of what the cloth believes
of its magus-like powers.

If fastening and unfastening are its nature,
it doesn't care about its nature.

It likes the caress of two fingers
against its slightly thickened edges.
It likes the scent and heat of the proximate body.
The exhilaration of the washing is its wild pleasure.

Amoralist, sensualist, dependent of cotton thread,
its sleep is curled like a cat to a patch of sun,
calico and round.

Its understanding is the understanding
of honey and jasmine, of letting what happens come.

A button envies no neighboring button,
no snap, no knot, no polyester-braided toggle.
It rests on its red-checked shirt in serene disregard.

It is its own story, completed.

Brevity and longevity mean nothing to a button carved of horn.

Nor do old dreams of passion disturb it,
though once it wandered the ten thousand grasses
with the musk-fragrance caught in its nostrils;
though once it followed—it did, I tell you—that wind for miles.

# Always She Reads the Same Translation

Always she reads the same translation,
and so over decades not one comma alters.

The letters' ascenders and descenders
travel no further
into their yearning toward spirit or body,
nor do they ever pursue that goal with a lessened passion.
The page gutters' margins do not fatten or thin.

Though she has had the poem
long by heart,
she takes the volume from the shelf each time.

Not once has the page grown a single gray hair;
and the title, at first in a foreign language,
remains in a foreign language—
but dear to her now as the furnishings of her own house,
strange only as a chair or table,
looked at sufficiently hard, is strange.

There are those who think the poem says something simple.
There are those who do not see themselves in its ink.

For her the poem—
or in the end, three words of it, just three—
is the gaze of a first lover on the body,
is an arc-welder's cutting torch showering sparks,
is a nightmare.

For these reasons, she keeps returning.
She is looking for something it looks for also, in her.

No lion's sudden tooth tearing the core,

it is the tooth of a rat gnawing.
It eats slowly and she lives, moving a little.

## Only When I Am Quiet and Do Not Speak

Only when I am quiet for a long time
and do not speak
do the objects of my life draw near.

Shy, the scissors and spoons, the blue mug.
Hesitant even the towels,
for all their intimate knowledge and scent of fresh bleach.

How steady their regard as they ponder,
dreaming and waking,
the entrancement of my daily wanderings and tasks.
Drunk on the honey of feelings, the honey of purpose,
they seem to be thinking,
a quiet judgment that glistens between the glass doorknobs.

Yet theirs is not the false reserve
of a scarcely concealed ill-will,
nor that other, active shying: of pelted rocks.

No, not that. For I hear the sigh of happiness
each object gives off
if I glimpse for even an instant the actual instant—

As if they believed it possible
I might join
their circle of simple, passionate thusness,
their hidden rituals of luck and solitude,
the joyous gap in them where appears in us the pronoun *I*.

# RED ONION, CHERRIES, BOILING POTATOES, MILK—

Here is a soul, accepting nothing.
Obstinate as a small child
refusing tapioca, peaches, toast.

The cheeks are streaked, but dry.
The mouth is firmly closed in both directions.

Ask, if you like,
if it is merely sulking, or holding out for better.
The soup grows cold in the question.
The ice cream pools in its dish.

*Not this,* is all it knows. Not this.
As certain cut flowers refuse to drink in the vase.

And the heart, from its great distance, watches, helpless.

As if suspended in alchohol
or the weightlessness of gravity's absence,
they float.

Neighboring bits bump, then part,
becoming nothing—
no name, no invitation, no refusal.

A bestiary of incoherent parts,
braying and babbling.
Clay arms attached to clay-tusked trunks or hooves.

A longing seems to hover near them.
*Sil. La. Pum.*

How close they draw to the real.

Which may or may not
lean toward them as well:
a lengthening bean-vine or clematis,
following the sun behind clouds.

Any moment, surely,
one will become *piano, dictionary, house-dress.*
Then *consolation, resolution, awe.*

If they hesitate a little longer, on that threshold,
be further patient.
Recognize slow-yieldingness as gift.

Let them linger as almost-meaning—
as *cluff of lisbirds, gliefy res-thrum, welted calf-folh*—
before the sorting and separations begin,
before they become *material, certainty, story.*

I haven't yet found the pronoun through which to touch it directly.
You may feel differently.
You may think you can simply reach through all the way
  with your hand, like petting the shoulder of an old dog, who, when
she can no longer stand, lies on her bed, watching her kingdom
  arriving and leaving, arriving and leaving, until at last
it only departs.
We want our lives and deaths to be like that—something formal, a kingdom.
  Filled with the sense of the manyness of existence. As the French say
"*Vous*" to that which cannot yet be made familiar.
They do this less and less these days, it seems.

I received a letter requesting that I invent a form, a task
you will think should be easy, but
it was not. The request simmered, month by month, half forgotten.
We have an agreement, the muse and I,
you see, about requests:
they have to come from her, or else be like
    those winter flies suddenly slow and loud in a house
    whose doors and windows have been long closed and locked.
    When the owners return, in spring, the small, dark bodies remain—
    evidence that something always happens.
    Even when there is nothing, something happens.

As with love. "Not here, not now," the heart protests.
Then the evidence: irrefutable, the low buzzing.

I have been wondering why there is no name for that part of poetry's music which is not rhythmic. It is simple to say "meter," "drumbeat," "stress"—but what is the other half called? Prosody, "sound," melopoeia—each covers both. Rhyme is merely a fraction; assonance, consonance, tune mean only themselves. Perhaps it is like the problem of horse and rider: Easy to have a horse with no rider, impossible to have a rider without, grazing somewhere nearby, a horse. Time exists without the scented, muscular body traveling through it, but no planet, parrot tick, leopard lives free of time. Even the purest singing signals a maculate conception, within an imagination schooled by passage. And so that part of poetry's music made by the untempered mouth, breath, and throat remains, without the measuring hoofbeat, uncapturable silence. A mockingbird's song heard in a mirror; the shadow a dog's night-barking leaves on the dark.

# All Evening, Each Time I Started to Say It

All evening, each time I started to say it,
something would interrupt.
It was not a thought so very large—
it could in fact have slipped through any window
cracked open a bit for air.
Yet each time I started to say it, at that table,
someone else would speak, the moment would pass.
After the fifth time this happened, I began to be amused.
*Runt-of-the-litter thought*, I thought, *unable to get to the tit*.
Then suddenly wanted to lift it up,
to feed it an eyedropper's measure of mare's milk,
some warmed sugar water, a little colostrum of badger.
It suddenly seemed to me the kind of thought,
not large, on which a life might turn.
There are many such: unheard, unspoken.
Their blind eyes open and close,
the almost audible valves of their hearts.
But all evening, each time I started to say it,
something would interrupt, the moment would pass.

# Dark-Grained, Surprisingly Heavy

Dark-grained,
surprisingly heavy in the hand,
larded with raisins.
Made of several flours and coarse-ground seeds.

"It freezes well," she said.
"A gift."
Then that she meant to share it.

The muse is like that, I thought, returning half.

The first slice I burned.
The second, eaten unbuttered from the toaster,
burned my tongue.

I have reached the time, it seems,
of looking outward.
Bread or startlement more of use than my own heart.

I lean from the window and hear the hawk's cry:
*Kyriiiiiiii. Kyrie Eleison.*
Even those sharp-taloned beings
summoning mercy, kneeling into the dive.

With every mouthful,
something more torn open.

Why is it so difficult to speak simply?

# In Praise of Coldness

"If you wish to move your reader,"
Chekhov wrote, "you must write more coldly."

Herakleitos recommended, "A dry soul is best."

And so at the center of many great works
is found a preserving dispassion,
like the vanishing point of quattrocento perspective,
or the tiny packets of desiccant enclosed
in a box of new shoes or seeds.

But still the vanishing point
is not the painting,
the silica is not the blossoming plant.

Chekhov, dying, read the timetables of trains.
To what more earthly thing could he have been faithful? —
Scent of rocking distances,
smoke of blue trees out the window,
hampers of bread, pickled cabbage, boiled meat.

Scent of the knowable journey.

Neither a person entirely broken
nor one entirely whole can speak.

In sorrow, pretend to be fearless. In happiness, tremble.

Even now,
decades after,
I wash my face with cold water—

Not for discipline,
nor memory,
nor the icy, awakening slap,

but to practice
choosing
to make the unwanted wanted.

# THE LIE

Like a moveable theme drawn into being by a great composer,
    who places it into one part of the music, then another,

sometimes folding or inverting it like shirting-fabric,
sometimes setting it upside down like a stone or a swarm of bees
    that knows neither top nor bottom,
        yet by balance remains recognizable and whole,
the old lie comes.

Its notes like white-faced cows looking back in strong starlight.

Difficult to say why this so pleases.
Perhaps it is not the outcome, but the listening,
    the being asked once more to listen.

# Happiness Is Harder

To read a book of poetry
from back to front,
there is the cure for certain kinds of sadness.

A person has only to choose.
*What* doesn't matter; just *that*—

This coffee. That dress.
"Here is the time I would like to arrive."
"Today, I will wash the windows."

Happiness is harder.

Consider the masters' description
of awakened existence, how seemingly simple:
*Hungry, I eat; sleepy, I sleep.*
Is this choosing completely, or not at all?

In either case, everything seems to conspire against it.

All summer you kept trying to answer the knocking.

Down the hill,
the new houses composed themselves,
first story, second story, roof.

Your own story stayed unvisited, unfurnished.
What lived there
was smaller than mouse-sized. Perhaps a cricket still moved.

The heart, wanting to waken,
drank its tiny cups of morning espresso.
One morning choosing a green cup,
the next morning yellow. Red. Blue. Then once again green.

All summer the heart circled the wheel of its colors.

What does it matter if now a dog wakes you,
night after night, in the dark?
Comes to the bed and stares until you open the door,
then goes out to start up a racket that no neighbor hears.

When Tu Fu turned forty,
he drank rice wine, dipped his cup over and over,
barked like a dog into wind.
Perhaps this dog is Tu Fu, still going on,
howling at time, at friends gone to the Yellow Springs.

Does he hunt some impossible answer —
beauty? or justice? — there in the outer dark of the world?
Or, more modern questioner,

hunt only the scented knock of a better question?

He is gone a long time.
Who stands in the doorway is you.
Still, waking is waking. It is good to have a companion.

The late stars shine in the cold, some red, some blue.

## Each Day I Choose from Among the Steepening Reminders

Each day I choose
from among the steepening reminders
of all I have failed to finish, failed to begin.
I open a right-hand cover and read the last page.

Phrases severe and perfect rise before me,
wrung from every extremity of joy and sleek-limbed loss.
Borges, Sinyavsky, Hadewijch, Sappho, Li Po.

More arrive each week, ink sharp as new hunger.

And these are only the books:
the thing already ambered, capable of waiting, turned to words.

Bought in a flea market,
cheaply,
because of one corner torn
as if it had caught
on a nail or been chewed by a dog.

For thirty years I carried it with me,
house to house, life to life.

Now I have had it repaired.

The colors are the same,
but the pattern is different.

The new fringe cut to the same
worn length as the old,
but a darkness where the line
of white hook-shapes is missing.

I had learned, it seems, to expect
the glimpse of underlying floorboards.

Change comes.

The repair is skillful, was needed.

Now only a different imperfection
has entered the weave.

But something in me has diminished.
A door the fates once opened
has been nailed closed and plastered over.
The white dust covers my hands.

# The Gallop

There are days the whole house moves at a gallop.
Bookshelves and counters, bottles of aspirin and oil,
chairs, saucepans, and towels.

I can barely encircle the neck
of a bounding pen with my fingers
before it breaks free of their notions;
open the door before the dog
of lop-eared hopes leaps through it;
pick up the paper before it goes up as kindling.

Barely eat before something snatches
the toast from my plate,
drains the last mouthfuls of coffee out of my cup.

Even these words—
before the blue ink-track has dried on the paper,
they've already been read
and agreed to or flung aside for others I don't yet know of,

and well before
I have dressed or brushed out the braid of my hair,
a woman with my own shadow
has showered and chosen her earrings, bought groceries
and fallen in love, grown tired, grown old.

Her braid in the mirror shines with new ribbons of silver,
like the mane of a heavy warhorse.
He stands in the silence as if after battle, sides heaving, spent.

# PILLOW

Some pillows are made of down, feathers,
and striped cotton ticking,
some of wool or dried herb flowers,
others of thought.

The thought of a good sandwich
in the lunch bag, for instance—
provolone slices and garden tomato,
a little Dijon and mayonnaise—can be a pillow,

comforting as the memory of being,
for one moment,
not entirely embarrassed to be human.

Able, say, to meet the gaze
of a cow or a horse with eyes neither arrogant
nor lowered, to offer a carrot
not as propitiation or bribe but simple friendship.

Friendship can be simple,
like the pillow of a horseshoe's lucky curve
above a door where it's needed.

"Here," I said to my friend when he was dying.
"Here," he replied.

There was nothing more to ask of one another,
though we spoke a while longer,
words like river pebbles, some black, some white,
wrapped in a handkerchief's tied-together purse.

I could not eat them,
so I put them under my pillow that night,

and slept well,
without dismay or turning,
though he would continue dying, though I would live.

His look, those days: plain as water, undeterred
by the ongoing disassemblage.
A little greedy, but also ready, prepared.

Whatever came, he told me, would be his own luck.

We held hands a time,
then together let go that touch,
together turned to our separate tasks,

like the two hands
of a person arranging the blankets and pillow
just so before sleeping,
settling the one day in order to enter the next.

# "Nothing Lasts"

"Nothing lasts"—
how bitterly the thought attends each loss.

"Nothing lasts"—
a promise also of consolation.

Grief and hope
the skipping rope's two ends,
twin daughters of impatience.

One wears a dress of wool, the other cotton.

# GREAT POWERS ONCE RAGED
## THROUGH YOUR BODY

Great powers once raged
through your body, waking and sleeping.
What remains?

A few words, your own or others'.
A freshened affection for silence and rest;
but also for lightning and wind,
familiar to you now as your own coat or shoes.

They lie on the closet floor
in the scent of paint and pinewood,
as if you had picked them out for yourself,
as if you had carried them home.

*"What could have happened, has happened."*
The sentence repeating itself in your ear
as a pear repeats itself, each time a little altered,
on every branch of the tree.

Chair, table, dishcloth, bowl—
each thing under your hand or your eyes
you regard now as ally, as friend.

And yet this hard-won composure
feels already a little simple, a little meek—
like a painting
of yellow houses or fields, before
the narrow slashes of red have been riveted in.

# "A Carbon-Based Life Form"

A person tired from happiness grows sober.

Another, worn through
by sadness, stumbles into a kind of joy.

It is like a dog alone in a house, barking to hear its own kind.

Nothing needs to be added. Yet we do.

# MINOTAUR

Once a minotaur,
a secret revealed becomes a rock,
a tree, a cow like any other.
Only the one who once held it, seeing it
thus diminished, strokes the rough bark or small ears,
leans against the silent, cold surface with sorrow,
remembers it in its former, fearsome glory.

We stood in the dark outside a door
and talked in the scent of jasmine.

Three women standing at the foot of—what?
One mountain of three lifetimes' lucks and losses,
the other actual and breathing, above us in the dark.

The year's new leaves and grasses were resting all around us.
Somewhere above us, deer were sleeping.
Bobcats, beetles, owls were sleeping.

We spoke of neither mountain.
We breathed in the scent of jasmine between words
whose meaning didn't matter.
Only the murmur mattered, going on.

It was night. Deer slept, and bobcats.
Our lives paused with us in the doorway, waiting.

# LADDER

A man tips back his chair, all evening.

Years later, the ladder of small indentations
still marks the floor. Walking across it, then stopping.

Rarely are what is spoken and what is meant the same.

Mostly the mouth says one thing, the thighs and knees
say another, the floor hears a third.

Yet within us,
objects and longings are not different.
They twist on the stem of the heart, like ripening grapes.

# BLUE WINDOW

In the dream, some believe, everything matters equally.

The protagonist who sits at the table
no more or less the dreamer's necessity than the table
or the small spoon she finds at rest in her left hand.

The clink of soup spoon stirred against soup bowl
no more nourishing or less nourishing than the red soup.
In the dream, the ears drink and drink—
how thirsty they must have been for that sound.

The legs of the table drink too, like lapping panthers,
four of them gathered companionably
around the legs of the woman holding the spoon,
as if a sudden, pure democracy, or a painter's peaceable kingdom.

As if the chorus reentering after the aria's close,
or a blue window opening out of a pale orange wall.

As if a durable assuaging.

As if the cell in the breast and not the breast,
or if the breast then that alone and not the woman,

though all things in the dream be equal,
not the woman,
neither the one who eats and listens

nor she mercifully, these minutes longer, dreaming.

# MUSLIN

"I never knew when he would come,"
  my friend said of her lover,
"though often it was late in the afternoon."

Behind her back the first plum blossoms
  had started to open,
few as the stars that salt the earliest dusk.

"Finally weeks would go by, then months,"
  she added, "but always I let him in.
It made me strong, you see,

"the gradual going without him.
  I think it taught me a kind of surrender,
though of course I hated it too."

Why he would appear or stay away
  she never fathomed—
"I couldn't ask. And that also seemed only good."

A small bird fluttered silent behind her left shoulder,
  then settled on some hidden branch.
"Do you ask the weather why it comes or goes?"

She was lovely, my friend, even the gray
  of her hair was lovely. A listening rope-twist
half pity, half envy tightened its length in my chest.

"When he came, you see, I could trust
  that was what he wanted.
What I wanted never mattered at all."

The hands on her lap seemed quiet,
even contented.
I noticed something unspoken begin to

billow and shimmer between us,
weightless as muslin,
but neither of us moved to lift it away.

# WALKER EVANS INTERIOR, 1936

From the photograph it's impossible to tell
whether one of the chair legs is short
or the floorboards sag.

But you can feel how every time
the woman comes in from the weather
and sits by the food safe
to unlace her cold boots and the day's mud-stiffness

she knows the sudden tock of shifting balance.
How the whole interior shudders and settles again.

I feel it now, traveling
through my own ease of thigh and light knock of seatbone
and into the simple good luck of my ribs.

The bump of a kind of hope against its lock,
or a hard kiss against her,
the kind you'd only miss after it stopped.

Like an ant carrying her bits of leaf or sand,
the poem carries its words.
Moving one, then another, into place.

Something in an ant is sure where these morsels belong,
but the ant could not explain this.
Something in a poem is certain where its words belong,
but the poet could not explain this.

All day the ant obeys an inexplicable order.
All day the poet obeys an incomprehensible demand.

The world changes or does not change by these labors;
the geode peeled open gives off its cold scent or does not.
But that is no concern of the ant's, of the poem's.

The work of existence devours its own unfolding.
What dissolves will dissolve—
you, reader, and I, and all our quick angers and longings.
The potato's sugary hunger for growing larger.
The unblinking heat of the tiger.

No thimble of cloud or stone that will not vanish,
and still the rearrangements continue.

The ant's work belongs to the ant.
The poem carries love and terror, or it carries nothing.

# SELF-PORTRAIT IN A BORROWED CABIN

One night eating potatoes pan-fried,
the next night baked, two nights later, mashed.
A hummingbird drives at the evening fuchsia,
still sunlit this far north.
Because I have seen this before, I think:
*My hummingbird is drinking.* And later, *my four-point buck*—
who also likes the red flowers.
If the hummingbird is thinking, *my pendant fuchsia,*
*my watching human,* I will not know it.
Then in broad evening brightness the raccoon
races its shadow across the mown grass.
Not *my raccoon*—it's Eleanor and Richard's, next door.
Each of us racing with him, making our own
for a little while, as travelers do, what is no one's.
Every third morning here I wake from another nightmare,
and still I find myself thinking: *paradise, bliss.*

# THE CONTRACT

The woman who gave me the rosebush
reminds me:
"Cut it back hard."

The stems resist.

Thorns and weedy twig-thickets
catch on jacket sleeve, on gloves.
Core-wood splinters green under the shears.

Impossible to believe
that so little left will lead to fragrance.

Still, my hands move quickly,
adding their signature branch by branch,
agreeing to loss.

# POEM WITH TWO ENDINGS

Say "death" and the whole room freezes—
even the couches stop moving,
even the lamps.
Like a squirrel suddenly aware it is being looked at.

Say the word continuously,
and things begin to go forward.
Your life takes on
the jerky texture of an old film strip.

Continue saying it,
hold it moment after moment inside the mouth,
it becomes another syllable.
A shopping mall swirls around the corpse of a beetle.

Death is voracious, it swallows all the living.
Life is voracious, it swallows all the dead.
Neither is ever satisfied, neither is ever filled,
each swallows and swallows the world.

The grip of life is as strong as the grip of death.

(but the vanished, the vanished beloved, o where?)

How empty the counter,
all her medicines
gone.

## A Scale Weighs the Outer World in Pounds and Ounces

A winch,
with its drag drum and hoist drum, is strong.

Grief is stronger,
yet weighs no more than the pattern
of leaf and sun on the bark of a tree.

Joy, too, is strong,
yet changes no more than the cloth of a curtain
pulled open rather than closed.

Emotion—handless and eyeless—
runs through the body like current through copper wire.
Equally innocent of its ends, equally voracious.

A scale weighs the outer world in pounds and ounces.
The sum does not alter,
whatever happens within and between us.

One will feel this as blessing, another as horror.

# BONE

The living dog
has found the old dog's toy.
She brings it to the kitchen,
the blue rubber a little cracked
from all that time outside.
My memories,
my counting and expectations,
mean nothing to her;
my sadness, though,
does puzzle her a moment.
Then she keeps on chewing.
Time's instruments are thumb piano,
oboe, ocarina, flute, and dog.
Its movements
run through her body flawlessly.
Only we sing with a catch in the throat.
She hears the thought. —"Catch?"
She's ready.

# MOMENT

A person wakes from sleep
and does not know for a time
who she is, who he is.

This happens in a lifetime
once or twice.
It has happened to you, no doubt.

Some in that moment
panic,
some sigh with pleasure.

How each kind later envies the other,
who must so love their lives.

The carrier, I read, is *Salmonella.*
It must be kept cold.
It must not be held long in the mouth
before it is swallowed.

It was given me taped to a gel pack.
Has it been chilled like this always?
I am to take one each two days
for a week, on an empty stomach.

I have opened it now, there
is no going back. The insert speaks of efficacy,
lack of side effects, proven safety.
Was it collected, fermented with care,

well inspected? How was it shipped?
There is no going back.
The capsule rests in my hand
like new love or a stinging insect.

# The Poet Looks at Her Poems

She looks at the pages, she lifts one
suddenly incomprehensible as Phoenician.

She looks at the pages:
now the world silent as beach stones, raw as peeled hedgehogs.

She looks at the pages and wonders
to whom that cold heart could belong.

She looks at the pages,
ponders the billowing sentiment of their tongue.

She looks at the pages: strangers.

She looks at the pages: vaguely familiar,
dogs she has passed in the street.

She looks at the pages: finds in them
many lost loves, some in the major key, some in the minor.

And so it continues, sheet after printed sheet:

    distant relatives, nursery school teachers,
    acquaintances wanted and not;
    ululations and whinnies, throat clearings, cheeps.

    Some with small inked corrections at the elbow or flank;
    new commas like tiny earrings, deletion-tattoos on the inner thigh.

The sign in their window:

"No one under eighteen unless doing laundry."

The directions important to read before their assembling:
"Insert flap A in slot C, then carefully invert."

Their red label-warning:
"Consult physician at once if symptoms persist."

She looks at the pages'
gray hairs at the part-line,
at their chin
whose small new doubling resembles hers.

These symptoms, she suspects, will persist.

The whole assemblage seems easily
carryable from room to room in the crook of one arm,
so she does.

She looks again, in the different—

She tucks flap B in slot G.

# Elephant Seals, Año Nuevo Preserve

They remind of the walnut's almost welded-in sweetness.
They remind of the unbribable cat.
They remind of the roof, its sloped unconcern for above or below.

Individual and silent, each thick-glassed bottle.
Clarified and complete-in-itself, each shoulder-hunched stone.

Consider an engine, enclosed in its alien hums and whistles.
Consider a two-ton beetle, clacking its varnished sheen.

Like an onion growing larger without any limit:
ungraspable, its umbilical sugars and heat,
its inner moistness wrapped in the thinnest of papers.
Three layers, four at most define it—
on one side rampantly onion, on the other impassive soil.

So it is with these groundfallen rainclouds,
these past ripe, prize-winning melons out-buckling their skin.

Though here, where one being ends, an equal begins.
Sometimes lying side by side like companionable rowboats,
sometimes touching with sensitive noses—
quick as hollow-boned plovers then, light as sand flies.

In every unknowable earth-fold, unknowable ardor.

What appears to be stubbornness,
refusal, or interruption,
is to it a simple privacy. It broods
its one thought like a quail her clutch of eggs.

Mosses and lichens
listen outside the locked door.
Stars turn the length of one winter, then the next.

Rocks fill their own shadows without hesitation,
and do not question silence,
however long.
Nor are they discomforted by cold, by rain, by heat.

The work of a rock is to ponder whatever is:
an act that looks singly like prayer,
but is not prayer.

As for this boulder,
its meditations are slow but complete.

Someday, its thinking worn out, it will be
carried away by an ant.
A *Mystrium camillae*,
perhaps, caught in some equally diligent,
equally single pursuit of a thought of her own.

# One Life Is Spent, the Other Spends Us

One life is spent, the other spends us.

Rarely, they touch—
like a cat for the first time meeting itself in a mirror.

In the world, mirrors are few.
The slightest wind dissolves them.

In a life, the moments of recognition are few.

Consciousness does not hate or love, it neither grieves nor longs.
Walking and breathing are not its nature.
It is.

Yet something passes and ends, grows wet in rain then dries,

and the small bowl of kibble empties into a delicate, spotted paw,
a tail slightly kinked, a preference for one windowsill
over another.

# AUGUST DAY

You work with what you are given—
today I am blessed, today I am given luck.

It takes the shape of a dozen ripening fruit trees,
a curtain of pole beans, a thicket of berries.
It takes the shape of a dozen empty hours.

In them is neither love nor love's muster of losses,
in them is no chance for harm or for good.
Does even my humanness matter?
A bear would be equally happy, this August day,
fat on the simple sweetness plucked between thorns.

There are some who may think, "How pitiful, how lonely."
Others must murmur, "How lazy."

I agree with them all: pitiful, lonely, lazy.
Lost to the earth and to heaven,
thoroughly drunk on its whiskeys, I wander my kingdom.

# BALANCE

Balance is noticed most when almost failed of—

in an elephant's delicate wavering
on her circus stool, for instance,
or that moment
when a ladder starts to tip but steadies back.

There are, too, its mysterious departures.

Hours after the dishes are washed and stacked,
a metal bowl clangs to the floor,
the weight of drying water all that altered;
a painting vertical for years
one morning—*why?*— requires a restoring tap.

You have felt it disappearing
from your own capricious heart—
a restlessness enters, the smallest leaning begins.

Already then inevitable,
the full collision,
the life you will describe afterward always as "after."

# IDENTITY

Decades after a man leaves the Church,
still he is called the priest.

Many years since she set down her bow,
a woman remains the cellist.

The one who seduced so many is content
now to sip her tea,
and still she is looked at with envy and hatred.

The one who held life and death
in his mouth
no longer speaks at all, yet still he is feared.

The unmoving dancer rehearses her steps.
Again, perfection eludes her.

Fate loosens its grip. The bruises stay.

# FOR HORSES, HORSEFLIES

We know nothing of the lives of others.
Under the surface, what strange desires,
what rages, weaknesses, fears.

Sometimes it breaks into the daily paper
and we shake our heads in wonder—
"Who would behave in such a way?" we ask.

Unspoken the thought, "Let me not be tested."
Unspoken the thought, "Let me not be known."

Under the surface, something that whispers,
"Anything can be done."

For horses, horseflies. For humans, shame.

# SPEED AND PERFECTION

How quickly the season of apricots is over—
a single night's wind is enough.
I kneel on the ground, lifting one, then the next.
Eating those I can, before the bruises appear.

# OPTIMISM

More and more I have come to admire resilience.
Not the simple resistance of a pillow, whose foam
returns over and over to the same shape, but the sinuous
tenacity of a tree: finding the light newly blocked on one side,
it turns in another. A blind intelligence, true.
But out of such persistence arose turtles, rivers,
mitochondria, figs—all this resinous, unretractable earth.

Hunger, fear, curiosity, desire—
these four
would have more than sufficed.

By what sudden lurch
of kindness
or small moment's inattention
were creation's fierce gods possessed,

to give us this supernumerary joy?

It is foolish
to let a young redwood
grow next to a house.

Even in this
one lifetime,
you will have to choose.

That great calm being,
this clutter of soup pots and books—

Already the first branch-tips brush at the window.
Softly, calmly, immensity taps at your life.

# Silk Cord

In the dream the string had broken
and I was trying to
pick out its beads among all others.

The large coral beads,
the beads of turquoise and ivory--
these were not mine.
Carved and ridged with color, burnished, weighty—
my hands passed over them without regret or pause.

The tiny ones,
of glass,
almost invisible against the white cotton bedspread—
these were mine.

The hole in the center
scarcely discernible as different from the bead itself,
the bead around it
scarcely discernible as different from the bed or floor or air—

with trembling fingers
I lifted them
into the jar my other hand cupped closely to one breast.

Not precious, merely glass, almost invisible.
How terrified I was at the thought of missing even one.

*While I live,* I thought, *they are mine to care for.*

Then wakened heavy with what I recognized at once
as an entirely warranted grief,

frantic for something plain and clear
and almost without substance,
that I myself had scattered, that I myself must find.

# THE SILENCE

One acquaintance says of another,
"I think he's a happy man,"
then pauses.

I see on his face what I also
am thinking,
and wonder what he is remembering,
inside our silence.

I am remembering a funeral,
friend after friend rising to speak
of the lost one.
I did not know him well,
yet still, by one thing he had told me,
wore fully our closeness.

Or perhaps it was even simpler—
to whom else could he say the truth?

I wondered, even then,
how many others attending knew also one thing.
Each secret separate, different,
leading its life now without him:
carrying laundry, washing the windows, straightening up.

As they do, perhaps, I would like to sit down now and rest.

I would like to ponder the flavor
of how much I know of others, how much I do not;
of what of me is known and what is not.

A conversation is overheard on a train, on an airplane,
and even Love cannot know the whole.

It sits in the row behind,
listening quietly to what it is able.
Then the green and red wing-lights blink out;
the train rounds the track's curve and is lost.

Love, also disappearing,
would like to tap the two murmuring ones on the shoulder.
Love would like to say to them,
"Speak more fearlessly— This is the only— Say what you can."

Politeness forbids it.

Love sits in the row behind,
and quietly listens.
Love lowers its stricken face so no one will see.

# SLEEP

Horses, yes.
Dogs, old ones especially.
People of course.
Even trees.

Planets, atoms do not.
A bacterium, a virus?
Unlikely.

Pens sleep
most of the time,
but awaken quickly—
one shake
or a few dry strokes suffice.

A fire sleeps by dark,
a cat by daylight,
each curled in a warming circle.
A rock lies still or tumbles,
but cannot sleep.

Does the wool
sleep along with its sheep?
The hoof with its cow?

The finger sleeps
and the ring does not—
what of the vow?

A woman touched by a man
pretends, sometimes,
to sleep,

for the pleasure of letting him think
that she awakens.

After, her thighs
sleep differently from before.

Sometimes the heart
goes sleepless or sleeps for years;
sometimes the mind.

I have tried to talk
with my sleep,
to ask it politely for this or that,
but it only averts its gaze.

"Go away," it says,
and, "Leave me alone."
As if without me
it could be anything at all.

Still, it knows who is slave,
who master.

And so I lavish on it
goosedown and soft cotton,
offer it sweetened milk
or wine,
tuck it into warm blankets
under a window opened just an inch.

Some speak
of entering sleep,
but it is sleep that enters us,
as a farmer, familiar,
confident, enters his field.

Night after night it tills and waters,
so that at times we awaken
buoyant,
other times in inexplicable grief.

And though the child
who refuses to sleep
is right perhaps to be inconsolable—
begging more time,
clutching her bear to her cheek—
she too will finally agree.

Joining the silent magpies
and tough-skinned conch and saguaro;
the swaying mule deer,
suspended pipefish,
and deep-sighing maple—

all who, drifting,
distal,
quilt the drowsy night-song of the mortal.

# CLOCK

There is no substance
that does not carry one inside it,
hands spinning
as the Fates were said to do.

Or, more truly, carry many:
in one body the clock of the knee
and the ankle-clock keep different times,
the swaying metronome of the breast ignores
the solstice curve of rib that supports it.

Nor does the body's clock
govern its soul's,
which may move more quickly or slower—
a divergence seen in some moods
as tragic, comic in others.

All clocks in themselves are serene.
It is their task to run down.

And so the clock of the tree
welcomes its beetles and lichens,
the clock of the house feasts with its termites.

And still the clock of the marrow
spills out its cells gone wrong
and the clock of the family falters, unoiled and forgotten.
The living clock of fallible springs runs
side by side with the death-clock of quartz,
and neither clock can touch the hands of the other.

Some clocks are indifferent and perfect,
others bend over as walking animals under strong wind.

Even the clock of blue, uprisen granite
carries within it
the cooling clock of its own erosion to gruss.
Whole ranges this way disappear, obeying their clocks,
while the clock of a grove of aspen,
in theory immortal,
still shivers each season's gold-leaf into the wind.

A wet dog comes into the kitchen to shake off her wetness.
The drops fall, then dry: a clock's ticking gone suddenly still.

The clock of a memory
not remembered is not stopped,
as the clock of a memory remembered is not stopped.

Neither do these clocks grow larger or smaller,
greater or lesser, more bitter or sweet.
They stay on their walls, their dashboards, their wrists.
There, they are called watches, as if observers,
as if that close to the body they could look back.

Clock of the bamboo dipper that fills with water
then clacks itself empty, unlistened to, year after year;
gravity egg-clock of turned-over three-minute sand;
clock of the isotope's half-life, of a spotted mare come into heat;
star-clocks of Stonehenge, of Chichén Itzá,
of the rotating earth-face that holds two numbers only, light and then dark.
Clock of a pickup's engine leaking its oil,
"Three weeks before she needs some, steady as clockwork."

They do not look back.
They do not look, concerned with neither our terrors nor joys.
Only the eye looks at them,
looks and looks while swimming its river of lubricant tears—
some shuddered in unconcealed loudness;

some whispered silent over the cheekbones and down the chin's crevice;
most—steady slipstream of life still living—held for all time.

The merest glimmer, blinked back almost unnoticed,
as the blinking of a watchface goes almost unnoticed, until it is gone.

# INK

Like all liquids,
it is sister to chaos and time:
wanting always
to lose itself in another,
visible only when held in embrace.

It is also like the aurochs
of ancient Europe,
reentering the world with reluctance—
at the threshold, marks of the scoring horns,
their curls, tip-blots, and scratchings.

Some of its substances:

Carbon of lampblack.
Lapis well-powdered.
Rust flakes milled fine.

Certain inks grip their surface,
others soak in.
Still others, like potters' glazes,
require baking—
the paper arrives warm then with its words,
a fresh bread seeded with poppies.

The tulip magnolia
writes first in white ink, then in green.
Each new twig blossoms as ink to the reading mind.

As with the squid's dark cloud
or the writings on certain moth-wings,
some inks are meant to disguise—

the eye of the hawk stares fiercely,
but where is the hawk?

Some glossy, brilliant, expounding,
others darkly impenetrable as sleep,
all consist of pigment, binder, and carrier.

Each part must be compatible with the others.
And so the glueing binder—
shellac, gum arabic, plastic, or resin—
must enter seamlessly
into the carrier's solvent.
In this, ink is like a metaphor well-made.

And like metaphor,
good ink has also its fragrance:
some smell of earth,
others are heady with spirits.

In itself ink is carrier, solvent,
and pigment to thought:
thought, entering ink,
equally transports, rushes, and stays.

Alcohol-based, oil-based, or water,
all inks must eventually dry,
releasing their words from the verb tense
of present-resilient to that of perfected past,

They settle weightless, meaningful as dust.

Until the reader—
an aromatic organic carrier
not unlike any other,
not unlike, say, fresh turpentine meeting old varnish—

redissolves them,
adds back the moistened eye, the moistened mind.

Then the drying and non-drying oils—
petroleum, soya—
unfasten their chemical binding.
The script-melisma unscrolls in the listening ear.

And again the impossible
happens with such ease it is almost unnoticed:

A radish once dipped
in salt and eaten is eaten once more.
A mountain walks in and out of its quantum of fog.
A woman of ancient China paints on her eyebrows.

Then each grain of that salt
passes again through the world-gate,
returned to the black gates of ink, which silently close.

# Metempsychosis

Some stories last many centuries,
others only a moment.
All alter over that lifetime like beach-glass,
grow distant and more beautiful with salt.

Yet even today, to look at a tree
and ask the story *Who are you?* is to be transformed.

There is a stage in us where each being, each thing, is a mirror.

Then the bees of self pour from the hive-door,
ravenous to enter the sweetness of flowering nettles and thistle.

Next comes the ringing a stone or violin or empty bucket
gives off—
the immeasurable's continuous singing,
before it goes back into story and feeling.

In Borneo, there are palm trees that walk on their high roots.
Slowly, with effort, they lift one leg then another.

I would like to join that stilted transmigration,
to feel my own skin vertical as theirs:
an ant road, a highway for beetles.

I would like not minding, whatever travels my heart.
To follow it all the way into leaf-form, bark-furl, root-touch,
and then keep walking, unimaginably further.

## About the Author

Jane Hirshfield's books of poetry include *Given Sugar, Given Salt; The Lives of the Heart; The October Palace; Of Gravity & Angels;* and *Alaya.* She is also the author of a collection of essays, *Nine Gates: Entering the Mind of Poetry,* and editor and co-translator of two collections, *Women in Praise of the Sacred: 43 Centuries of Spiritual Poetry by Women* and *The Ink Dark Moon: Love Poems by Ono no Komachi and Izumi Shikibu, Women of the Ancient Court of Japan.* She is the recipient of fellowships from the Guggenheim and Rockefeller foundations, the Poetry Center Book Award, the Bay Area Book Reviewers Award, the Commonwealth Club of California's Poetry Medal, and Columbia University's Translation Center Award, among other honors. Her work has been featured in the *Best American Poetry 2001* and *Pushcart Prize* anthologies as well as in many periodicals, including *The Atlantic Monthly, The Nation, The New Republic,* and *The New Yorker.* A former visiting associate professor at the University of California, Berkeley, and lecturer at the University of San Francisco, she currently teaches at Bennington College in the MFA Writing Seminars.